NATURAL GAS

by Rebecca Rowell

ENERGY LAB:
NATURAL GAS

CHERRY LAKE PUBLISHING • ANN ARBOR, MICHIGAN

Published in the United States of America
by Cherry Lake Publishing
Ann Arbor, Michigan
www.cherrylakepublishing.com

Printed in the United States of America
Corporate Graphics Inc.
January 2013
CLFA10

Consultants: Timothy R. Carr, Marshall Miller Professor, Department of Geology and Geography, West Virginia University; Marla Conn, reading/literacy specialist and educational consultant

Editorial direction:
Lauren Coss

Book design and illustration:
Christa Schneider

Photo credits: Shutterstock Images, cover, design element (all), 1, 8, 11, 13, 19, 21, 23; Yuri Arcurs/Shutterstock Images, 5; Jubal Harshaw/Shutterstock Images, 7; iStockphoto, 15; Red Line Editorial, 17; Kelly Boreson/Shutterstock Images, 25; Monkey Business Images/Shutterstock Images, 27

Library of Congress Cataloging-in-Publication Data
Rowell, Rebecca.
  Natural gas / Rebecca Rowell.
    pages cm. – (Energy lab)
  Audience: 7-8
  Audience: K to grade 3
  Includes index.
  ISBN 978-1-61080-895-8 (hardback : alk. paper) – ISBN 978-1-61080-920-7 (paperback : alk. paper) – ISBN 978-1-61080-945-0 (ebook) – ISBN 978-1-61080-970-2 (hosted ebook)
  1. Natural gas–Juvenile literature. I. Title.

TP350.R69 2013
553.2'85–dc23

                        2012031310

Cherry Lake Publishing would like to acknowledge the work of The Partnership for 21st Century Skills. Please visit www.21stCenturySkills.org for more information.

TABLE OF CONTENTS

You are being given a mission. The facts in What You Know will help you accomplish it. Remember the clues from What You Know while you are reading the story. The clues and the story will help you answer the questions at the end of the book. Have fun on this adventure!

Your mission is to investigate natural gas as an energy source. People use natural gas every day to heat their homes, cook, and even fuel their cars. Businesses and industries use it too. Natural gas might play a huge role in the way we use energy in the future. To understand why, you need to learn more about natural gas. Where does natural gas come from? When did people begin using it as fuel? What do we use it for today? How do we get this fuel? What will we use natural gas for in the future? Check out the facts in What You Know. Then begin your mission to find out more about this important energy source!

WHAT YOU KNOW

★ Natural gas is a **fossil fuel**. It forms from **organic** materials buried underground for millions of years.
★ All fossil fuels, including oil, coal, and natural gas, cause pollution. Their supply is also limited.
★ Natural gas is an important energy resource worldwide.

People use natural gas every day for cooking, heating their homes, and more.

★ Natural gas creates less pollution than oil and coal.

★ Natural gas makes up about 25 percent of U.S. energy use.

★ Some people believe we should increase the amount of natural gas we use compared to other energy sources.

Ashley Banday wants to learn more about natural gas. She is meeting with scientists and other natural gas experts. Reading Ashley's journal can help you in your own research.

I want to get started on my research by learning more about what natural gas is and how we use it. My next-door neighbor, Mr. Dixon, is a middle school science teacher. I think he might be able to help me, so my mom and I stop by his house on a Saturday.

"Ah, natural gas," he says. "You've just mentioned one of my favorite fuels! Natural gas has been around a long time. In fact, most of the natural gas we find today is millions of years old. It's buried deep inside the earth."

He explains that natural gas is a fossil fuel like oil and coal. Fossil fuels are made from organic material.

"Believe it or not, natural gas actually comes from sea creatures," Mr. Dixon says. "These tiny sea creatures lived hundreds of millions of years ago. When they died, these creatures ended up at the bottom of the ocean. Over a really long time—many millions of years—layer upon layer of sand and **silt** covered their remains. They became buried deeper and deeper inside the earth. There, heat and pressure changed the buried creatures into oil, coal, and gas."

Mr. Dixon tells me people in the Middle East and China discovered natural gas thousands of years ago. But it took quite a while before anyone used natural gas as an energy

Natural gas comes from the fossils of tiny sea creatures that lived hundreds of millions of years ago.

source. Fredonia, New York, was the first U.S. city to use natural gas commercially. In 1821, gunsmith William Hart dug the first U.S. natural gas well outside Fredonia. People living there began using the gas for cooking. They also used it to light their homes and businesses.

After oil, natural gas is the second-most-used energy source in the United States. One-fourth of U.S. energy was supplied by natural gas in 2011.

"You probably use natural gas in your own house," Mr. Dixon says. "Natural gas can heat homes, power clothes

dryers and water heaters, and provide energy to your
backyard grill. Natural gas can also power businesses and
factories. Almost 40 percent of natural gas used in the
United States produces electricity. We also use natural gas
to make products such as plastic and fertilizer. And our
uses for natural gas are still growing! Natural gas is even
starting to power different types of transportation."

Mr. Dixon explains that most vehicles run on
gasoline created from oil. Gasoline causes pollution when
burned in cars, trucks, and buses. The pollution releases

Some three-wheeled taxis in Thailand
run on natural gas.

DRIVING WITH NATURAL GAS

Natural gas costs less than gasoline and diesel. It also gives off less pollution when burned. Approximately 112,000 vehicles in the United States and almost 15 million around the world run on natural gas. Natural gas vehicles (NGVs) use one of two types of natural gas. Compressed natural gas (CNG) is natural gas under pressure. Liquefied natural gas (LNG) is compressed gas that has been cooled into a liquid. CNG vehicles are useful for driving short distances. They serve as taxis, postal trucks, street sweepers, and more. LNG vehicles are good for driving longer distances.

carbon dioxide into the atmosphere. Too much carbon dioxide traps the sun's energy like heat in a greenhouse. This causes a gradual increase in Earth's temperature, known as global warming. Natural gas releases some carbon dioxide when it is burned. But it gives off much less carbon dioxide than other fossil fuels, making it a cleaner source of energy. Natural gas vehicles (NGVs) are better for the environment than regular vehicles.

I think I understand how we use natural gas today. But I'm still not sure exactly what natural gas is. And how do we turn it into energy? ★

Today, I am meeting with Dr. Alexis Quentin. She is a chemist at a university in California. Dr. Quentin studies what things are made of and how different substances interact. I explain to her that I know where natural gas comes from. Now I want to know exactly what it is.

"Natural gas is a combination of elements," says Dr. Quentin. "It's mostly methane, which is a type of gas called a **hydrocarbon**. Hydrocarbons are made of two elements: hydrogen and carbon." She points to a chart on the wall that's called the periodic table of elements. The table has many squares. Each square has one or two letters, plus

H_2O

Chemists use formulas to describe substances. For example, you might have heard of "H-2-O." That's the chemical formula for water. The formula tells us there are two hydrogen (H) atoms and one oxygen (O) atom in a molecule of water. Natural gas is mostly methane and ethane. Methane and ethane are hydrocarbons. They are made of only hydrogen and carbon (C) atoms. The chemical formula for methane is CH_4. The formula for ethane is C_2H_6. What does that tell you?

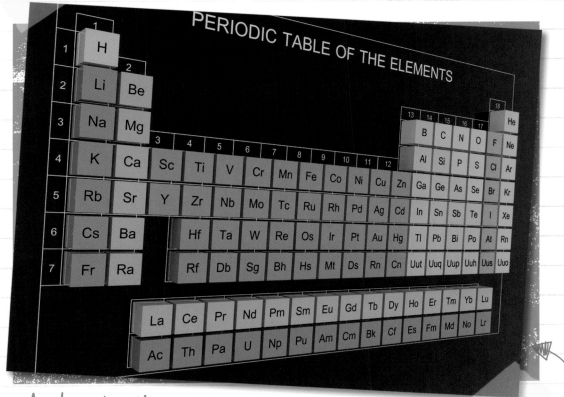

An element is the most basic form of a substance. The periodic table lists information about every known element.

some numbers. The table has different colors too. Hydrogen and carbon are two of the squares on the table.

"Are there other kinds of hydrocarbons in natural gas?" I ask.

"Yes," Dr. Quentin says. "Natural gas is a mixture of hydrocarbons, but it has non-hydrocarbons too. Other gases, including carbon dioxide, helium, hydrogen, and nitrogen, are usually mixed in with the hydrocarbons."

"Wow," I say. "Natural gas really isn't one thing. It's lots of things."

Next, Dr. Quentin tells me about some of the physical properties of natural gas. I already know that natural gas is **flammable**. It catches fire when my mom turns on a burner on our stove.

Dr. Quentin tells me natural gas is odorless and colorless. You can't see it or smell it. It also doesn't create any smoke when it burns. Dr. Quentin says there's a lot more to know about natural gas. She suggests I meet with a geologist, someone who studies rocks and the earth. ★

Natural gas works as a fuel because
it is extremely flammable.

Now I know where natural gas comes from, a bit about what it's made of, and some of its properties. Next, I want to learn about how we get natural gas from the earth.

Today, I am meeting with Dr. Shelby Wong, a geologist in Mississippi. She starts by telling me a little bit about natural gas.

"Natural gas is classified one of two ways," she says. "It is either associated or non-associated. Associated gas is found with oil. The oil and gas are associated. This means they are companions. This type of natural gas often contains liquid, so it's also called wet gas."

Dr. Wong explains that non-associated gas occurs by itself. It doesn't contain liquids, so it is known as dry gas. Sometimes non-associated gas is found inside sand or shale, a type of rock. Just like associated gas, non-associated gas is often deep inside the earth.

Dr. Wong tells me technology helps find natural gas. She says sometimes scientists also use evidence on Earth's surface to find natural gas below ground. When she goes into the field to look for evidence of natural gas, Dr. Wong is looking for a land formation called an anticlinal slope.

Geologists look for evidence of natural gas buried deep below the earth's surface.

"Anticlinal slopes occur in places where the earth is folded," Dr. Wong explains.

"You mean like a shirt is folded?" I ask.

"Exactly!" she says. "A dome results when this happens. History has shown these slopes are more likely than other places to have **reservoirs** of oil and natural gas."

Dr. Wong tells me scientists also rely on seismology to find natural gas. Seismology is the study of earthquakes and man-made vibrations in the earth. Small instruments called geophones are often set up in areas being studied for possible natural gas. Geophones measure vibrations created by humans. In the past, scientists used dynamite to make the ground vibrate. Today, they drive heavy trucks over the area. Geophones measure the vibrations the trucks create to see if natural gas is present.

"The vibrations bounce off different rocks in different ways," Dr. Wong says. "Think of bouncing a ball. It will bounce one way on a sidewalk and another way on grass."

GAS TRAPS

Natural gas is often found deep inside the earth in a rock formation called a gas trap. The trap's arched shape makes it possible for natural gas to form. A gas trap has several layers of rock. The source rock is the source of the natural gas. The reservoir rock is the rock natural gas seeps into. The reservoir rock is solid. But it is also porous so gas can flow through it. A layer of water, oil, and gas sits between the source rock and the reservoir rock. The cap rock is at the top of the formation. The cap rock is less porous than the reservoir rock. It holds everything inside the rock. The cap rock also called a seal.

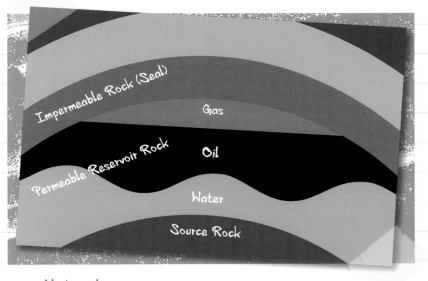

Natural gas is often found in a rock formation called a gas trap.

Labels in image: Impermeable Rock (Seal), Permeable Reservoir Rock, Gas, Oil, Water, Source Rock

"So, you don't measure natural gas, you measure vibrations against rocks?" I ask.

"Right! This helps identify where traps might be located. A trap is an underground rock formation that contains natural gas."

Dr. Wong says when a fuel company thinks it has found a natural gas deposit, it will usually drill an exploratory well.

"That's really the only way to know for sure if natural gas exists in an area. If natural gas is discovered, the well will be developed for production."

More goes into finding natural gas than I thought! But I wonder, what do we do with the gas once we find it? ★

Now that I understand how scientists detect natural gas, I want to learn more about how they get it out of the ground. Today, I'm in Louisiana meeting with Ben Salieri. He is an engineer with an energy company. He oversees drilling at the well I'm visiting. Mr. Salieri says this well is a vertical well.

"Hi there," Mr. Salieri says. "I hear you want to learn about natural gas production."

Mr. Salieri explains vertical wells are made using rotary drilling. A giant drill bit is spun into the ground.

"Have you ever seen someone drill a hole in a piece of wood?" he asks. "We're doing the same thing but on a much larger scale."

"After a well is drilled, there are a few steps to finishing it," Mr. Salieri says. "First, metal well casing is inserted into the well. The casing has several layers. It strengthens the sides of the well. It also keeps gas from seeping out and other matter from getting inside. Next, a metal wellhead is added. This is the part of the well you can see above the ground. The wellhead controls the rate of the gas removal. It also prevents leaks."

Giant vertical drills access natural gas below the ground.

Mr. Salieri says the well we're at is getting dry gas. This gas flows on its own. It simply needs to be accessed by the well to escape. Wet gas comes from an oil well.

"The method this well uses is just one way to get at natural gas," Mr. Salieri says. "Some wells use a method called hydraulic fracturing, or fracking. Once the well is dug, millions of gallons of liquid are pumped into it. The watery mixture pounds the shale. It causes it to fracture, or crack. The natural gas escapes through the cracks and can be collected by the well. This method allows us to get at a lot of natural gas we might not otherwise be able to reach. However, many people are concerned about hydraulic fracturing's effect on the environment."

Mr. Salieri goes on to tell me that once natural gas is retrieved, it needs to be refined, or cleaned. Once it is refined, the natural gas is ready for use. Pipelines take natural gas from the well to the processing plant and then

DO YOU SMELL ROTTEN EGGS?

Natural gas benefits people and businesses by providing energy, but it can be harmful too. Natural gas is explosive. It is also poisonous to people and animals when they breathe in too much of it. Natural gas has no color, odor, or taste. This means people may be unaware when there is a gas leak. A spark could easily turn a leak into an explosion. Because of this, utility companies add a chemical called mercaptan to natural gas during the production process. It makes natural gas smell bad—like rotten eggs.

Ships transport natural gas across oceans.

to places the natural gas is needed—usually cities. Ships take natural gas overseas.

Mr. Salieri explains that natural gas goes into storage for future use or to the utility company. The utility company has its own system of pipelines that distributes natural gas to customers.

There are a lot of steps to getting natural gas ready for use. I thank Mr. Salieri for showing me around. On to my final stop! ★

My final stop is in Nevada. I am meeting with Brendan Pryse. He is a professor of geochemistry at the local university. He is interested in the future of natural gas.

Thanks to my research, I understand there are many pros and cons to natural gas as an energy source. One of the biggest cons is that natural gas is a **nonrenewable** fossil fuel. We are going to run out at some point. I ask Professor Pryse how long natural gas will last.

"Well, that depends who you ask," he responds. "Some experts think natural gas could be the future of U.S. energy. In 2011 alone, natural gas production grew by more than 7 percent from the previous year. Until then, that was the biggest increase ever in one year."

Professor Pryse tells me scientists don't agree about how long our natural gas stores will last. Some experts think there's enough natural gas to last 60 years. Other experts say our natural gas stores will last closer to 100 years. Technology has improved how we locate and drill it. Hydraulic fracturing is a big part of that technology.

Professor Pryse explains that another source for natural gas is being studied. Gas hydrates are solids made of gas and water molecules. They are located in

Thousands of miles of pipelines transport natural gas around the world.

out-of-the-way places. We find them in the Arctic and below the ocean floor. Researchers estimate gas hydrates in the Gulf of Mexico could provide enough natural gas to fuel the United States for more than 1,000 years.

"One hundred years and 1,000 years are only estimates though," Professor Pryse says. "Fracking is a new process, and gas hydrates are still being studied."

"Isn't more gas a good thing?" I ask.

ABOUT THE AUTHOR

Rebecca Rowell has a master of arts degree in publishing and writing from Emerson College. She has edited a variety of nonfiction books for children. In addition to writing about natural gas for young readers, she has written about Iraq, Switzerland, and pioneer aviator Charles Lindbergh.

ABOUT THE CONSULTANTS

Tim Carr has been interested in geology since before he was late for third grade but was saved by sharing his fossils collected on the way. He has worked around the world as a petroleum geologist for 30 years.

Marla Conn is a reading/literacy specialist and an educational consultant. Her specialized consulting work consists of assigning guided reading levels to trade books, writing and developing user guides and lesson plans, and correlating books to curriculum and national standards.